Dunstanburgh Castle – a symbol of past conflict between the Scots and English.
Right: Tyne bridges cross the river between Newcastle and Gateshead.

NORTH-EAST ENGLAND

Graeme Peacock

MYRIAD

Above: perched on its huge rock Bamburgh Castle dominates the pretty village below, clustered around its wooded green.
Left: in 1902 Lindisfarne Castle on Holy Island was bought by Edward Hudson, the founder of *Country Life* magazine.
He employed Sir Edwin Lutyens to restore the building and convert it into a home.

Left: the Farne Islands are owned by the National Trust. They consist of a group of islands 2.5 miles (4km) off the fishing village of Seahouses; of these, islands 15 and 28 are visible depending on the state of the tide, and they form one of Britain's most important seabird sanctuaries. The closest island is Inner Farne and the furthest out, at 4.4 miles (7km) from the shore, is Knivestone.

It was from the distinctive red and white Longstone lighthouse on one of the outer Farne islands that Grace Darling and her father rowed out to rescue the survivors of the shipwrecked *Forfarshire*. Flashing once every 20 seconds night and day the lighthouse was built between 1825 and 1826. The chapel on Inner Farne is built on the site of St Cuthbert's Oratory and was restored in the 19th century. Lit by a beautiful stained-glass window the serene interior is decorated with oak panelling, screens and stalls brought from Durham Cathedral.

The sun sets over the cobles nestling in the harbour of Beadnell. The huge sweep of glorious Beadnell Bay make it one of the most popular holiday beaches in the area.

Left and above: Alnwick Castle. Known as "the Windsor of the North", the rolling fields and "natural" landscape of Alnwick were the work of the famous gardener Lancelot "Capability" Brown who laid out the grounds in the 18th century. The Grand Cascade is one of the high points of the castle's magnificent gardens.

On the southern side of the Aln estuary, Alnmouth Cross marks the site of the original village church of Alnmouth.

Above: the Grecian-style Belsay House was built by Sir Charles Monck in 1817, employing some of the finest craftsmen of the day. Belsay Castle is in the grounds of the beautifully maintained estate.

Above: Wallington Hall. This magnificent Palladian-style country house is set amongst 100 acres of parkland. The castle that previously stood on the site was owned by the famous Fenwick family of Northumberland.

Right: the sedate river Wansbeck flows through Morpeth, one of the major market towns of Northumberland. The footbridge shown here is built on the abutments of the medieval bridge destroyed in 1832.

Below: sited on a loop of the river Coquet, Warkworth was originally a wooden fortress built after the Norman Conquest. During the Middle Ages the wooden structure was gradually replaced by strong stone battlements.

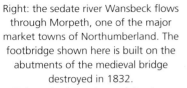

Right: Hadrian's Wall was begun in AD 122 and stretched 73.5 miles (117km) from Wallsend on the river Tyne to the shores of the Solway Firth. A great deal of the middle section of the wall is largely intact and along its length are the ruins of a number of forts and milecastles. The Romans made use of the steep slopes of the countryside, including the escarpment at Whin Sill, as a major defensive element in the construction and siting of the wall.

Left: Housesteads is the best-preserved example of a Roman fort in Britain. It held a garrison of around 1,000 men, most of whom were German auxiliaries. By the 13th century, Housesteads became a hiding place for reivers (cross-border raiders) and the cattle they had stolen.

Above: the Vicar's pele tower at Elsdon was built around 1400 and has walls 9ft (3m) thick. The battle of Otterburn was fought nearby and some of the dead were buried under St Cuthbert's, Elsdon's parish church.

Left: the rolling Cheviot Hills straddle the Scottish-English border and stretch across the northern half of Northumberland ending in the valley of the river Coquet to the south.

Below: with its sloping green shaded by sycamores, Rothbury is known as the capital of Coquetdale. It is a popular destination for visitors many of whom come to explore the Simonside Hills to the south of the town.

Left: to the north and south of Blyth's harbour entrance are beautiful wide open beaches backed by sand dunes. Like many other ports in this area, Blyth owes its present size to the development of the coal industry. Nine wind turbines stretch along the East Pier.

Right: lit up at twilight, St Mary's Lighthouse makes a beautiful reflection in the rock pools at low tide and also reveals the causeway which crosses the dangerous rocks surrounding the island. Built in 1898 and some 120ft (36.5m) high, the lighthouse has a birdwatching hide and visitor centre. From the light's platform the view of the coast slips away southwards towards Whitley Bay, Cullercoats and the mouth of the Tyne.

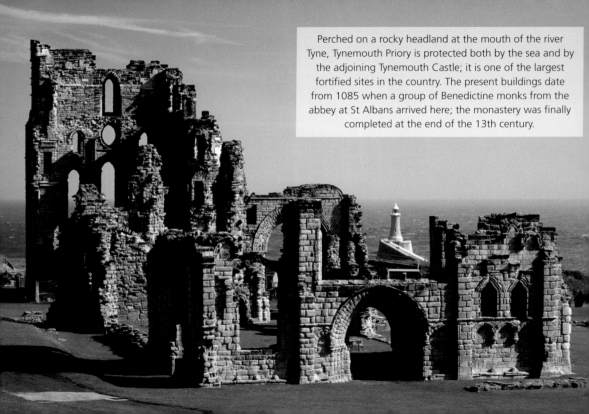

Perched on a rocky headland at the mouth of the river Tyne, Tynemouth Priory is protected both by the sea and by the adjoining Tynemouth Castle; it is one of the largest fortified sites in the country. The present buildings date from 1085 when a group of Benedictine monks from the abbey at St Albans arrived here; the monastery was finally completed at the end of the 13th century.

Above: Cullercoats. The brightly-painted lifeboat station is a much-loved feature of the beach of this seaside town. In the late 19th century many artists, including Winslow Homer, flocked here; they became known as the "Cullercoats Group".

Above and right: the bridges that link Newcastle and Gateshead hold a special place in the history of the north-east. The Swing Bridge opened in 1876 and was designed to allow large ships to pass upriver. The High Level Bridge, opened in 1850, is one of the most important structures in the history of Britain's railways. Opened by George V in 1928 the Tyne Bridge is now associated with the mass of runners crossing it as part of the Great North Run. The Millennium Bridge (right) opened in 2001. It links Newcastle Quay with the Sage and Baltic arts centres on the Gateshead side. Nicknamed the "blinking eye", the bridge can be raised in only four minutes to allow ships to pass underneath.

Newcastle's Grey Street is named after Earl Grey, prime minister between 1830-34. He is celebrated in a monument sited at the top of Grainger Street. The twice life-size statue was sculpted in 1838 by Edward Hodges Bailey, who was also responsible for Nelson's statue in Trafalgar Square.

Right: the castle keep and St Nicholas's Cathedral. The keep is all that remains of the "new castle" that gave Newcastle its name. The cathedral is named after St Nicholas, the patron saint of sailors and boats.

Below: the Great North Museum: Hancock opened in 2009 following a £26m refurbishment. Its collections come from a variety of sources including Newcastle University's Museum of Antiquities, the Natural History Society of Northumbria and the Society of Antiquaries of Newcastle upon Tyne.

Left above: bathed in a blue light that seems to represent the waters of the Tyne, Newcastle's Civic Centre reflects much of the history and culture of this great city.

Left: the Theatre Royal in Grey Street has a distinctive portico with six massive Corinthian columns.

Above: the dramatic Law, Business and Design School buildings at the University of Northumbria are clad in stainless steel mesh frames to reduce over-heating on sunny days.

Right: the Angel of the North. Overlooking the A1 near Gateshead, Antony Gormley's iconic sculpture has become a firm favourite since its installation in 1998.

Left: this distinctive red-and-white lighthouse is on the coast road in Whitburn. Built in 1871 it is now a fascinating museum of the life and workings of a Victorian lighthouse.

Below: four miles east of Hadrian's Wall, Arbeia Fort guarded the entrance to the river Tyne. Constructed around AD160 as a supply depot for the 17 forts along the wall, the west gate has been reconstructed as a museum.

Right: the Marsden Rocks are situated on a beautiful stretch of coast just south of the mouth of the Tyne.

Left: Sunderland's Winter Garden houses a superb botanical collection of over 1,500 plants of 146 species in naturalistic settings under a single-span 98.5ft (30m) dome. The Garden is linked to Sunderland's remodelled museum and the upgraded and re-landscaped Mowbray Park in the city centre. Built in 1929 the Wearmouth Bridge (below) crosses the river Wear linking Sunderland with Hylton and Monkwearmouth on the north side of the river. The *Shadows in Another Light* sculpture lies just upstream from the bridge.

Begun by Bishop William of Calais in 1093, Durham Cathedral is an outstanding example of Romanesque architecture. The cathedral has been a centre for pilgrimage throughout its 900-year history. It contains the tombs of St Cuthbert, the saintly seventh-century bishop of Lindisfarne and that of the Venerable Bede, the first English historian, which were placed there in 1370. One of the most beautiful features of the cathedral today is the huge rose window with its central core depicting Christ surrounded by the apostles; it was created in the 15th century and reconstructed in the 18th.

Left: Durham Castle is a fine example of the Norman motte and bailey style of fortification. A strategic element in William the Conqueror's plan to pacify the north, building began in 1072 with a circular keep on top of the hill overlooking the town.
Below: Durham's cobbled Market Place.
Right and below right: the open air museum at Beamish was set up in 1970 and tells the story of the people of the north-east of England at two important points in their history – 1825 and 1913.

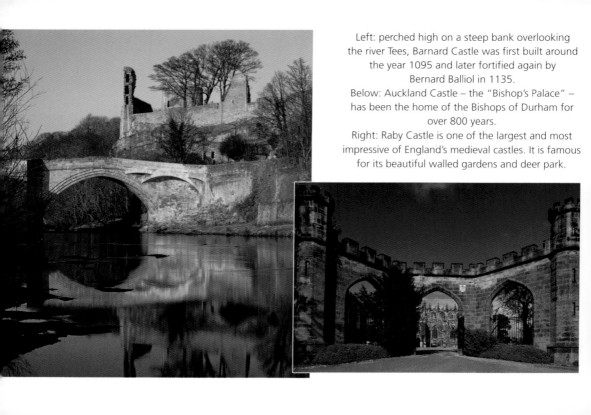

Left: perched high on a steep bank overlooking the river Tees, Barnard Castle was first built around the year 1095 and later fortified again by Bernard Balliol in 1135.

Below: Auckland Castle – the "Bishop's Palace" – has been the home of the Bishops of Durham for over 800 years.

Right: Raby Castle is one of the largest and most impressive of England's medieval castles. It is famous for its beautiful walled gardens and deer park.

Left and above: Bowes Museum in Barnard Castle originated in a private foundation created between 1862 and 1875 by John and Josephine Bowes.
Above right: Lumley Castle is a magnificent building set within nine acres of parkland, overlooking the river Wear.
Right: the ruins of Egglestone Abbey lie in the grounds of Egglestone Hall.

Left: the Upper Tees valley is an area of rolling countryside and windswept moorland dotted with handsome market towns. Its many beauty spots include the dramatic waterfalls at Low Force, High Force and Cauldron Snout.

Right: opened in 2009, the Infinity Footbridge in Stockton-on-Tees is a key element in the redevelopment of the north bank of the river. Just downstream, the Tees Barrage has created a large area of water for sports, fishing and recreation.

Left: the famous Transporter Bridge that dominates Middlesbrough's riverside skyline was designed to allow tall ships to pass beneath. The bridge has a unique system that ferries cars and pedestrians across the Tees. A travelling compartment, like a section of roadway, hangs by wires from a carriage that runs along the girders.

Above and left: the Historic Quay at the centre of Hartlepool's marina development is a reproduction of an 18th-century seaport. Dominating the marina area are the triple masts of HMS *Trincomalee*. Built of teak in India in 1817 she is the oldest fighting ship still afloat in the country. In 2010, the Tall Ships Race with its majestic sailing boats visited the port.